Pebble® Plus
Bilingüe/Bilingual

Patrones en la naturaleza/Patterns in Nature

Hibernar/
Hibernation

por/by Margaret Hall

Traducción/Translation: Dr. Martín Luis Guzmán Ferrer
Editor Consultor/Consulting Editor: Dra. Gail Saunders-Smith

Consultor en contenidos/Content Consultant:
Dr. Ronald Browne, Associate Professor of Elementary Education
Minnesota State University, Mankato, Minnesota

Capstone press®

Mankato, Minnesota

Pebble Plus is published by Capstone Press,
151 Good Counsel Drive, P.O. Box 669, Mankato, Minnesota 56002.
www.capstonepress.com

1 2 3 4 5 6 13 12 11 10 09 08

Library of Congress Cataloging-in-Publication Data
  Hall, Margaret, 1947–
    [Hibernation. Spanish & English]
    Hibernar / por Margaret Hall = Hibernation / by Margaret Hall.
    p. cm. — (Pebble Plus. Patrones en la naturaleza = Pebble Plus. Patterns in nature)
    ISBN-13: 978-1-4296-2371-1 (hardcover)
    ISBN-10: 1-4296-2371-3 (hardcover)
    1. Hibernation — Juvenile literature. 2. Sleep behavior in animals — Juvenile literature. I. Title. II. Series.
  QL755.H3518 2009
  591.56'5 — dc22   2008001206

Summary: Simple text and photographs introduce hibernation and how some animals prepare for and
    experience hibernation each year — in both English and Spanish.

Editorial Credits
Heather Adamson, editor; Katy Kudela, bilingual editor; Eida del Risco, Spanish copy editor;
    Kia Adams, designer; Jo Miller, photo researcher/photo editor

Photo Credits
Corbis/George McCarthy, 7, 21 (dormouse peering from hole and dormouse hibernating in nest); Hans Dieter
    Brandi/Frank Lane Picture Agency, 21 (dormouse eating berry); Hal Beral, cover (bear catching fish);
    Kennan Ward, 1, 11; Arthur Morris, cover (bear eating); zefa/E. & P. Bauer, cover (bear sleeping)
Dwight R. Kuhn, 13
Nature Picture Library/Colin Preston, 21 (dormouse on bramble)
NHPA/Anthony Bannister, 17
Peter Arnold/Deborah Allen, 19; S. J. Krasemann, 9
Photo Researchers Inc./Anne Fournier, 15
Shutterstock/Juerg Schreiter, backcover
SuperStock, 5

Note to Parents and Teachers

The Patrones en la naturaleza/Patterns in Nature set supports national science standards related to earth and life science. This book describes and illustrates hibernation in both English and Spanish. The images support early readers in understanding the text. The repetition of words and phrases helps early readers learn new words. This book also introduces early readers to subject-specific vocabulary words, which are defined in the Glossary section. Early readers may need assistance to read some words and to use the Table of Contents, Glossary, Internet Sites, and Index sections of the book.

Table of Contents

Tabla de contenidos

Why Hibernate?

Winter weather can be cold, cold, cold. Food is hard to find. Every winter, some animals stay alive by hibernating.

¿Para qué hibernar?

En el invierno el tiempo puede ser friísimo. Es difícil encontrar comida. En invierno, algunos animales se mantienen vivos hibernando.

5

Hibernating animals take a long, sleepy rest. They breathe slowly. Their hearts beat slowly too. They need less food for energy and heat.

Los animales que hibernan descansan adormilados durante mucho tiempo. Respiran muy despacito. Sus corazones también laten despacio. Así necesitan menos comida para tener energía y calor.

True hibernators, like bats, sleep
snuggled in for weeks without
waking. They don't eat. They
don't even go to the bathroom.

Los que hacen hibernación
profunda como los murciélagos,
duermen acurrucados durante
semanas sin despertarse. No
comen. Ni siquiera van al baño.

9

Getting Ready

Animals eat extra food before they hibernate. Bears get very fat in fall. They won't eat much during winter.

Hay que prepararse

Los animales guardan comida extra antes de hibernar. Los osos engordan mucho durante el otoño. No comerán mucho durante el invierno.

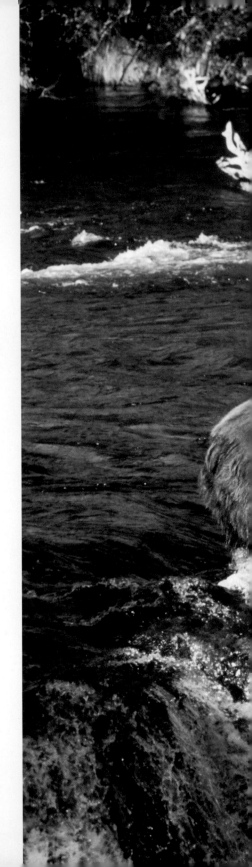

Some animals store up food
near their beds. Chipmunks
wake up and search for
a snack of hidden nuts.
Then they go back to sleep.

Algunos animales almacenan
comida cerca de sus camas.
Las ardillas se despiertan y comen
las nueces que escondieron.
Después se vuelven a dormir.

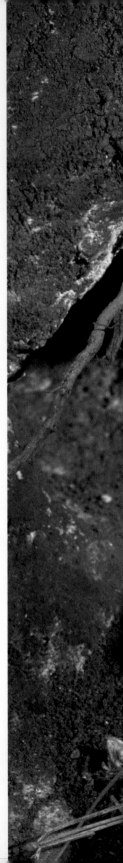

13

A Place to Rest

Groundhogs hibernate
underground in burrows.
Squirrels rest in nests
made of leaves.

Un lugar para descansar

Las marmotas hibernan
bajo tierra en madrigueras.
Las ardillas descansan en
nidos de hojas.

Frogs dig down deep and
sleep tucked in the mud.
Snakes curl up together
in caves.

Las ranas escarban muy hondo
en el lodo y ahí duermen
acurrucadas. Las serpientes
se enrollan juntas en cuevas.

Finally, the cold winter months
end and spring comes again.
Hungry animals leave their
winter beds to look for food.

Finalmente, los fríos meses
de invierno terminan y llega
la primavera una vez más.
Los animales hambrientos dejan
sus camas invernales para
buscar comida.

It's a Pattern

Hibernating is one of nature's patterns. When winter returns, animals will hibernate once again.

Se forma un patrón

Hibernar es uno de los patrones de la naturaleza. Cuando regrese el invierno los animales volverán a hibernar.

**Getting Ready/
Prepararse**

**Finding a Den/Encontrar
una madriguera**

**Leaving the Den/
Dejar la madriguera**

**Hibernating/
Hibernar**

Glossary

burrow — a tunnel or hole in the ground made or used by an animal

energy — the strength to do active things; food is needed to make energy in living creatures.

hibernate — to spend winter in a sleepy resting state without much activity

pattern — something that happens again and again in the same order

true hibernator — a hibernating animal that spends much of the winter in a sleeplike state and does not wake for weeks at a time; true hibernators have low body temperatures and heart rates; small mammals such as dormice and bats are true hibernators.

Glosario

la energía — fuerza para poder estar activo;
la comida es necesaria para crear energía
en los seres vivos.

hibernación profunda — estado parecido al sueño
en el que algunos animales se sumen la mayor parte
del invierno y del que no despiertan durante semanas.
La temperatura del cuerpo de estos animales baja
y el ritmo del corazón es más lento. Mamíferos
pequeños como los lirones y los murciélagos hacen
hibernación profunda.

hibernar — pasar el invierno adormilado en estado
de descanso casi sin actividad alguna

la madriguera — túnel o agujero en la tierra que
hace o utiliza un animal

el patrón — algo que se repite una y otra vez en
el mismo orden

Internet Sites

FactHound offers a safe, fun way to find Internet sites related to this book. All of the sites on FactHound have been researched by our staff.

Here's how:

1. Visit *www.facthound.com*

2. Choose your grade level.

3. Type in this book ID **1429623713** for age-appropriate sites. You may also browse subjects by clicking on letters, or by clicking on pictures and words.

4. Click on the **Fetch It** button.

FactHound will fetch the best sites for you!

Index

Sitios de Internet

FactHound te brinda una manera divertida y segura de encontrar sitios de Internet relacionados con este libro. Hemos investigado todos los sitios de FactHound. Es posible que algunos sitios no estén en español.

Se hace así:

1. Visita *www.facthound.com*

2. Elige tu grado escolar.

3. Introduce este código especial **1429623713** para ver sitios apropiados a tu edad, o usa una palabra relacionada con este libro para hacer una búsqueda general.

4. Haz un clic en el botón **Fetch It**.

¡FactHound buscará los mejores sitios para ti!

Índice